EDINBURG

THE CITY AT A GLAN

CW00621181

New Town
With its elegant Georgian terr
streets and manicured garde.
New Town is urban-planning perfection.

Melville Monument
Architect William Burn based this 1823 tribute
to Viscount Melville, aka 'the uncrowned King
of Scotland', on Trajan's Column in Rome.
At 41m, it looms over the New Town.
St Andrew Square

The Royal Scottish Academy
Re-opened in 2003, this building hosts world-
class exhibitions. The next-door Scottish
National Gallery (T 624 6200) displays art
from the Renaissance to the late 19th century.
The Mound, T 225 6671

Princes Street Gardens
Avoid the manic crush of shoppers along
Princes Street's main drag with a detour
through this pretty, peaceful park.

Scott Monument
George Meikle Kemp's 61m monument in
honour of Sir Walter Scott was unveiled in
1846. Some see it as an example of neo-Gothic
greatness, others as a weird space rocket.
East Princes Street Gardens

The Balmoral
Opened in 1902 as The North British Hotel,
this building links the architecture of the
Old Town with the neoclassicism of the New.
1 Princes Street, T 556 2414

Calton Hill
Climb this magnificent incline to marvel
at the breathtaking views and the tower
celebrating Nelson's 1805 Trafalgar victory.
See p013

INTRODUCTION
THE CHANGING FACE OF THE URBAN SCENE

If looks alone were the measure of a city, the Scottish capital would surely rank among the finest in the world. The dizzyingly romantic cobbled streets and medieval architecture of the Old Town are astonishingly intact, while the Georgian splendour of the New Town's broad streets and sweeping terraces is enough to give the first-time visitor goosebumps. But don't think for a minute that this is a city trading solely on its beauty; get to know it, and you'll discover it has a sharp, witty personality to match.

Edinburgh is a centre for the arts (and not just in August when it hosts one of the largest cultural festivals in the world). Home to an impressive range of galleries and theatres, it boasts a respected university, and a slew of bookish cafés. But just because the city is well read, it doesn't mean it goes to bed early. Edinburgh's pubs are renowned for their relaxed licensing hours and its bars have learned how to mix a decent cocktail or two. And let's not forget that it still puts on the biggest New Year's Eve party in Europe.

Devolution in 1999 brought a new-found confidence and the city has been moving forward ever since. Huge sums have been spent on sprucing up the former port of Leith, renovating national art galleries and – somewhat less successfully – bringing trams to the city centre. Visit now and you'll find more fine-dining restaurants, slick nightspots and exciting architecture than ever before. Today's Edinburgh does a lot more than just pose and look good.

ESSENTIAL INFO
FACTS, FIGURES AND USEFUL ADDRESSES

TOURIST OFFICE
Edinburgh and Scotland Information Centre
3 Princes Street
T 0845 225 5121
www.edinburgh.org

TRANSPORT
Bus
Lothian Buses
T 555 6363
Car hire
Hertz
10 Picardy Place
T 0870 846 0013
Chauffeur service
WL Sleigh Ltd
Unit 11
Turnhouse Road
T 339 9607
www.sleigh.co.uk
Taxi
City Cabs
T 228 1211
There are plenty of taxi ranks in
Edinburgh city centre and black cabs
can safely be hailed on the street

EMERGENCY SERVICES
Emergencies
T 999
Late-night pharmacy
Boots
48 Shandwick Place
T 225 6757
Open until 8pm, Monday to Friday;
6pm on Saturdays; 5pm on Sundays

CONSULATES
US Consulate General
3 Regent Terrace
T 556 8315
www.usembassy.org.uk/scotland

POSTAL SERVICES
Post office
8-10 St James Centre
T 0845 722 3344
Shipping
UPS
30 South Gyle Crescent
T 0845 787 7877

BOOKS
**Edinburgh: A Guide to Recent
Architecture** by Johnny Rodger (Batsford)
Exit Music by Ian Rankin (Orion)
The Prime of Miss Jean Brodie
by Muriel Spark (Penguin Classics)

WEBSITES
Architecture/Design
www.edinburgharchitecture.co.uk
Art
www.nationalgalleries.org
Newspaper
www.scotsman.com

EVENTS
Edinburgh Festival Fringe
www.edfringe.com
Edinburgh International Book Festival
www.edbookfest.co.uk

COST OF LIVING
**Taxi from Edinburgh Airport
to city centre**
£18
Cappuccino
£2.20
Packet of cigarettes
£6.50
Daily newspaper
£1
Bottle of champagne
£35

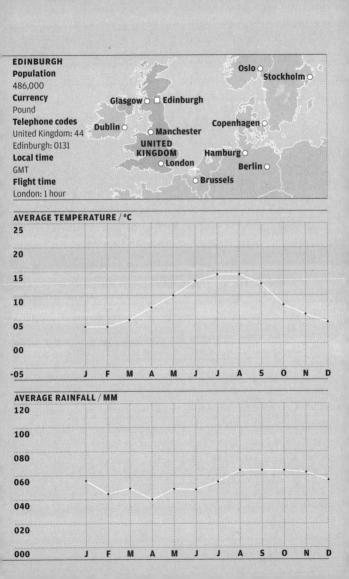

EDINBURGH
Population
486,000
Currency
Pound
Telephone codes
United Kingdom: 44
Edinburgh: 0131
Local time
GMT
Flight time
London: 1 hour

Oslo ○
Stockholm ○
Glasgow ○ □ Edinburgh
Dublin ○
Copenhagen ○
Manchester ○
UNITED KINGDOM
Hamburg ○
London ○
Berlin ○
Brussels ○

AVERAGE TEMPERATURE / °C

25												
20												
15												
10												
05												
00												
-05	J	F	M	A	M	J	J	A	S	O	N	D

AVERAGE RAINFALL / MM

120												
100												
080												
060												
040												
020												
000	J	F	M	A	M	J	J	A	S	O	N	D

NEIGHBOURHOODS
THE AREAS YOU NEED TO KNOW AND WHY

To help you navigate the city, we've chosen the most interesting districts (see below and the map inside the back cover) and colour-coded our featured venues, according to their location; those venues that are outside these areas are not coloured.

LEITH

Irvine Welsh's 1993 novel, *Trainspotting*, put the city's downtrodden port on the map. Two decades on and, although some rough edges remain, Leith is transformed. Galleries, waterfront bars and cafés are booming. At the heart of the area's regeneration is food. Leith is home to Edinburgh's holy trinity of Michelin-starred restaurants: Martin Wishart (54 The Shore, T 553 3557), The Plumed Horse (see p040) and The Kitchin (see p058).

SOUTHSIDE/NEWINGTON

This residential area between Bruntsfield Links and Holyrood Park is the city's least characterful zone. But it is home to the Pleasance (60 Pleasance, T 556 6550) and Festival (13-29 Nicholson Street, T 529 6000) theatres, music venue The Queen's Hall (85-89 Clerk Street, T 668 2019), the Royal Commonwealth Pool (see p068), several university buildings and Foster + Partners' Quartermile development.

NEW TOWN

This UNESCO World Heritage Site was designed in 1767 by a young Edinburgh-born architect named James Craig. The grand Georgian terraces and elegant neoclassical details have been meticulously maintained. Originally intended as a purely residential area, the New Town now boasts boutique hotels, such as The Howard (see p017), and several luxury department stores (see p080).

OLD TOWN

The city's core of medieval architecture and cobbled wynds dates back to the 12th century. Another UNESCO World Heritage Site, it is centred around the Royal Mile, which leads to the domineering Edinburgh Castle (see p010). To the south lies the Continental-style boulevard Grassmarket, lined with lively cafés and pubs. The area teems with ghost tours and tat shops, but it's impossible not to be impressed by all the historic details on show.

WEST END/TOLLCROSS/BRUNTSFIELD

The West End is not as pretty or charming as the Old or New Towns, but it does host several key arts venues, including Usher Hall (Lothian Road, T 228 1155). To the south-west, Tollcross has a somewhat seamy side to it, but emerging from this scruffy charm is Bruntsfield. Formerly a quarantine zone for plague victims, it now boasts boutiques, delis and handsome Victorian tenement buildings.

CANONGATE

Essentially the lower part of the Royal Mile, this district is steeped in history and tourist attractions, including John Knox House (see p073) and the Hopkins Architects-designed Our Dynamic Earth exhibition (Holyrood Road, T 550 7800). Since the arrival of the architecturally bold Scottish Parliament (see p070), opposite Holyrood Palace (Canongate, T 556 5100), Canongate has become a must-visit.

LANDMARKS

THE SHAPE OF THE CITY SKYLINE

Climb any of Edinburgh's reputed 'Seven Hills', look down at the metropolis beneath and you'll see that the city is quite a staggering landmark in itself. The sheer lack of 20th-century development in the centre means that, on a clear day, as you look out past the Gothic spires and blackened turrets to the dramatic coastline edging the Firth of Forth estuary, it really is a sight to behold.

In terms of city highlights, no one building shouts 'landmark' louder than <u>Edinburgh Castle</u> (overleaf). Built on top of a craggy escarpment as a medieval stronghold, it dominates the skyline and was the seat of Scottish royalty until the 17th century. It is the point from which the rest of the city has grown, and is an essential navigational tool. A pinnacle of the old city, it also acts as a striking contrast to Edinburgh's 18th- and 19th-century architecture.

This 'newer' development takes in the poignant and much-loved National Monument on Calton Hill (see po13), while more ornate buildings such as <u>McEwan Hall</u> (see po12), which was completed in 1897, show the extravagance that was lavished on Edinburgh's architecture during the Victorian age. Further evidence of this can be found if you take the short drive out to the Forth Rail Bridge (see po14). A masterpiece of engineering, this magnificent steel structure is as admired by locals as it is by visitors, having earned the nickname, the 'Eiffel Tower of Scotland'.

For full addresses, see Resources.

Edinburgh Castle
The sheer impact of the castle's presence can't fail to impress. Perched on Castle Rock, it housed Scotland's royal family until 1603, when James VI became James I of England. Today, it serves as a garrison for the British Army. A tourist magnet it may be, but one whose majesty surpasses that of most you'll see.
Castle Hill, T 225 9846, www.edinburghcastle.gov.uk

McEwan Hall

Edinburgh's students have long chuckled at the irony of graduating in a building with the same name as the beer that often served as the biggest distraction from studying for their degrees. Irony aside, the university was fortunate that prosperous Scottish brewery owner William McEwan financed the building of this semicircular neoclassical amphitheatre. Completed in 1897, it was the most flamboyant design of architect Sir Robert Rowand Anderson, who was also responsible for the Scottish National Portrait Gallery on Queen Street (see p034). If you like the extravagance of the exterior, William M Palin's interior is equally impressive.

Bristo Square

National Monument

The top of Calton Hill, with its grassy slopes and panoramic views, is probably one of the first places a local will take you. Yet despite its popularity and central location, the peak, reached via a steep staircase climbing up the hill from Waterloo Place, is a delightfully peaceful spot to spend half an hour or so. Next to the Nelson Monument, you'll see the bizarre site of this acropolis-style folly, designed by English architect Charles Robert Cockerell and Scotsman William Playfair. Modelled on the Parthenon in Athens and dedicated to those who died in the Napoleonic Wars, its construction began in 1824 but was never completed. At the time, it was seen as a national scandal. Today, it only adds to the lyrical feel of this characterful place.
Calton Hill

Forth Rail Bridge

It is perhaps indicative of Edinburgh's good fortune that although it was hardly touched by the Industrial Revolution (the city remained essentially professional), it still benefited from the most expensive, most beautiful feat of Victorian British engineering. The Forth Rail Bridge was designed by Benjamin Baker and Sir John Fowler and was completed in 1890. Linking Edinburgh and Fife, the cantilevered steel structure rises imperiously from the Firth of Forth, stretching 2.5km across the estuary. Despite the popular myth that repainting the bridge is a never-ending task, the job is due for completion in 2012. Trainspotting in Edinburgh may have new meaning thanks to Irvine Welsh, but as far as the hobby goes, there's no better place to do it than here.
Queensferry, www.forthbridges.org.uk

HOTELS

WHERE TO STAY AND WHICH ROOMS TO BOOK

For such a small city, Edinburgh attracts a huge number of visitors. At Hogmanay and during the Festival, there's notoriously no room at the inn, but booking well ahead is highly recommended over the rest of the summer as well. The grand Georgian residences in the New Town have made perfect boutique hotels, but with only a handful of rooms in each, they fill up fast. For this kind of intimate accommodation, The Howard (opposite) is one of the best options, while others, such as One Royal Circus (see p028), offer posh B&B-style service. Or stay at an actual B&B, in the chic, welcoming, albeit out-of-the-way 94DR (see p018). If good facilities and a central location top your priorities, choose the five-star The Scotsman (see p029) or The Balmoral (1 Princes Street, T 556 2414).

If you crave more contemporary surroundings, The Glasshouse (see p024) offers a modern take on the traditional Scottish interior, with large rooms and plenty of outside space, while Tigerlily (see p030) is best for party animals. Newcomer Hotel Missoni (p026), is one of two Matteo Thun-designed residences from the Italian fashion house. This one has an enviable location on George IV Bridge (the other is in Kuwait). The city also swirls with rumours of two controversial hotel projects: a conversion of the former Odeon cinema by Make Architects, and a redevelopment of the Royal High School by Gareth Hoskins. 'Wait and see' is the message. *For full addresses and room rates, see Resources.*

Dear Reader, books by Phaidon are recognized worldwide for their beauty, scholarship and elegance. We invite you to return this card with your name and e-mail address so that we can keep you informed of our new publications, special offers and events. Alternatively, visit us at **www.phaidon.com** to see our entire list of books, videos and stationery. Register on-line to be included on our regular e-newsletters.

Subjects in which I have a special interest

☐ General Non-Fiction ☐ Art ☐ Photography ☐ Architecture ☐ Design

☐ Fashion ☐ Music ☐ Children's ☐ Food ☐ Travel

	Mr/Miss/Ms	Initial	Surname

Name ⊔⊔⊔⊔⊔⊔⊔ ⊔ ⊔⊔⊔⊔⊔⊔⊔⊔⊔⊔⊔⊔⊔⊔

No./Street ⊔⊔⊔⊔⊔⊔⊔⊔⊔⊔⊔⊔⊔⊔⊔⊔⊔⊔⊔⊔⊔⊔

City ⊔⊔⊔⊔⊔⊔⊔⊔⊔⊔⊔⊔⊔⊔⊔⊔⊔⊔⊔⊔⊔⊔

Postcode/Zip code ⊔⊔⊔⊔⊔⊔ Country ⊔⊔⊔⊔⊔⊔⊔⊔⊔

E-mail ⊔⊔⊔⊔⊔⊔⊔⊔⊔⊔⊔⊔⊔⊔⊔⊔⊔⊔⊔⊔⊔⊔

This is not an order form. To order please contact Customer Services at the appropriate address overleaf.

Please delete address not required before mailing

PHAIDON PRESS LIMITED

Regent's Wharf

All Saints Street

London N1 9PA

UK

PHAIDON PRESS INC.

180 Varick Street

New York

NY 10014

USA

Return address for USA and Canada only

*Return address for UK and countries
outside the USA and Canada only*

The Howard

Staying here comes a close second to actually living in one of the Georgian apartments that line the New Town's avenues. Set on one of the area's most splendid streets, The Howard comprises three townhouses. Eighteen rooms, each named after a local street, are elegantly decked out but with plenty of home comforts, as in the Abercromby Suite (above). Every effort is made to create a 'non-hotel' atmosphere: you receive a key rather than a card, there's no booming air conditioning, the windows actually open and you're not bombarded by branding. Coupled with personal touches, such as your own butler and a cup of tea with your wake-up call, this attention to detail makes The Howard a model boutique hotel.
34 Great King Street, T 557 3500, www.thehoward.com

94DR

One of the best features of this 21st-century B&B is also the worst – its location. Set on a busy road in the Southside, a 10-minute ride from the centre, what it lacks in convenience 94DR makes up for in the sense of calm you get from staying at arm's length from the hordes. Amid the torrent of tartan that rampages through the city's guesthouses, Paul Lightfoot and John MacEwan's elegant townhouse has style. Fresh flowers grace its tiled entrance hall, cooked-to-order breakfasts are seasonal, there's an honesty bar, and attention to detail is such that showers have taps set to one side so you don't get a wet arm when you switch them on. The Bowmore Room (pictured) is our key of choice.
94 Dalkeith Road, T 662 9265, www.94dr.com

Prestonfield

This stunning 17th-century building on the edge of Holyrood Park, 15 minutes by cab from the city centre, was home to the Dick-Cunyngham family for three centuries. A hotel for 50 years, it has hosted guests such as Oliver Reed and Joan Collins. In 2004, it was bought by local restaurateur and hotelier James Thomson of The Witchery (see p022), who has turned it into something of a lavish folly. Each of the 23 rooms and suites, including the splendid Allan Ramsay Suite (above), is decked out with sleigh beds, velvet drapes and an indecent amount of heavy silk, and while it may not be to our taste, it does make us smile. If you are a minimalist, stay away, but for a decadent weekend, Prestonfield is hard to beat. Make sure you enjoy a meal in the opulent Rhubarb Restaurant (opposite).
*Priestfield Road, T 225 7800,
www.prestonfield.com*

The Witchery

If you're looking for eccentricity, opt for one of the eight theatrical suites located at the top of a winding stone staircase above James Thomson's celebrated restaurant of the same name. This is Gothic glamour at its extreme, each of the rooms boasting antiques and curiosities, opulent four-posters draped in velvet, roll-top baths for two and complimentary champagne. Forget wi-fi, plasma screens and power showers, The Witchery is all about romance. Think Versace does Victoriana and you're some way to imagining the lust den that is the Old Rectory – the suite of choice for Michael Douglas and Catherine Zeta-Jones when they're in town. Alternatively, opt for the Library Suite (right), with its leather-bound tomes, bathroom behind a secret door and wonderful views across The Royal Mile. *Castlehill, The Royal Mile, T 225 5613, www.thewitchery.com*

The Glasshouse

This project may have involved renovating the Lady Glenorchy church to within an inch of her life, but The Glasshouse has been a celebrated architectural achievement since it opened in 2003. Only the Gothic facade of the church remains, with a huge glass-and-steel structure welded to the back. The 65 rooms are pretty pared down, but what they lack in cosy romance, they more than make up for in comfort. The only decision you need make is whether to opt for front- or back-facing accommodation. Rooms at the front, including the Suites (opposite), have balconies overlooking the city, while those at the back, such as the Executive Room (above), have access to the roof garden and views to Calton Hill.
2 Greenside Place, T 525 8200,
www.theetoncollection.co.uk

Hotel Missoni

Though you won't find many clues to its presence (unless you count the doormen), slip between two colossal ceramic vases into the world's first Missoni hotel and you'll be met by a genuine buzz. The lobby bar is the closest Edinburgh gets to Miami, manned by cute-as-a-button staff and serving a sharp line in cocktails. Upstairs is Cucina, a modern Italian restaurant developed in collaboration with Giorgio Locatelli. A small spa offers Eve Lom and Natura Bissé treatments. Against a bold backdrop, heavy on the brand's trademark technicolour zigzags, the Missoni caters for tech-loving guests, with free in-room wi-fi, iPod docks and Nespresso machines. Best beds in the house? Room 507, with its killer view of the castle, or the luxe penthouse Suite D'Argento (right).

1 George IV Bridge, T 220 6666, www.hotelmissoni.com

One Royal Circus

Husband-and-wife team Mike and Susan Gordon moved into this elegant townhouse in 1998. Ten years and two children later, they concluded that it was better suited to entertaining guests, so they now run it as a B&B. The five well-designed rooms and apartments are simple but luxurious: beds are dressed with Frette cotton sheets and goosedown duvets, while each en suite boasts top-to-toe limestone tiling and top-of-the-range fittings. But it is the rest of the house that really sets this residence apart from any other hotel in the city. At your disposal are a bar, a large kitchen, sitting room, games room and gym, not to mention the striking main hall (above) and staircase. Best of all, there's no sign outside to announce this is a hotel. *1 Royal Circus, T 625 6669, www.oneroyalcircus.com*

The Scotsman

This gleaming five-star bears many traces of its former tenant, *The Scotsman* newspaper. The panelled boardroom, for example, is now a grand conference room, while the basement, which used to house the printing presses, works perfectly as a spa, with its stainless-steel pool, large gym and treatment areas. Many of the rooms, including the Editor's Office and the drawing room, with wood panelling and tall windows, are little changed. Up in the turrets, in what was once the advertising office, is the spectacular, if poky, Penthouse Suite. We suggest you opt instead for the two-floored Director's Suite, Room 801 (above), which has a tweed-draped canopy bed upstairs and a cosy living room downstairs.
20 North Bridge, T 556 5565,
www.thescotsmanhotel.co.uk

Tigerlily
This rock'n'roll hotel makes no attempt
at self-restraint, much like its cocktail
bar and club, Lulu, in the basement.
But the 33 rooms are more than just
a place to lay your head after one
too many, and are, in fact, very chic.
For pure decadence, reserve one
of the two Georgian Suites (pictured).
125 George Street, T 225 5005,
www.tigerlilyedinburgh.co.uk

24 HOURS

SEE THE BEST OF THE CITY IN JUST ONE DAY

If you heed only one piece of advice when in Edinburgh, it would be to wear comfortable (and, most of the time, warm) shoes. While there's no shortage of taxis around for late nights and the inevitable cloudbursts, if you don't put in the legwork you'll miss out on what makes this capital so impressive. Short cuts through its cobbled streets and hidden closes will reveal tucked-away art galleries, as well as inconspicuous shops selling beguiling wares. Equally, it could be the promenade along the newly developed docks at Leith or the sharp climb to admire one of the city's many breathtaking views that will lodge in your mind.

Luckily, Edinburgh is wonderfully compact and there are plenty of excellent places to fuel up as you plot your winding route. Start your day with a great Scottish breakfast or some delicious pancakes at Urban Angel (opposite), after which you'll be ready to tackle the city's resurgent art scene on a high at the newly renovated Scottish National Portrait Gallery (see p034). For lunch, stroll around the corner to The Dogs (see p036), the leader of a pack of restaurants in rude health. A short walk past North Bridge brings you to the imaginative installations of the Ingleby Gallery (see p038). Come nightfall, stay in the centre for a soirée at Castle Terrace (see p039), a French-inspired restaurant in the shadow of the castle, from Tom Kitchin, Leith's Michelin-starred supremo. *For full addresses, see Resources.*

10.00 Urban Angel

After witnessing the crowd that gathers outside this basement café at the weekend, you could be forgiven for thinking that something illegal must be going on inside, and the quality of the pancakes here does verge on the illicit. Here, as in a sister venue in Forth Street (T 556 6323), owner Gilly MacPherson has hit on a simple formula – a sleek but cosy café serving top-notch food at a decent price. Order a free-range omelette or organic porridge with heather honey, and feel smug about your responsible consumerism – almost all the ingredients are Fairtrade, organic or locally sourced. Featuring a polished flagstone floor and simple contemporary wooden furniture, the decor is also spot-on.

121 Hanover Street, T 225 6215,
www.urban-angel.co.uk

11.30 Scottish National Portrait Gallery

Reinvigorated in 2011 by Glasgow's Page \Park firm after a two-year, £17.6m refurb, and closer to architect Sir Robert Rowand Anderson's original 1899 designs than it was for much of the 20th century, the SNPG now allows visitors access to three floors, and a larger showcase of its portrait and photography collections in new spaces such as the Contemporary Gallery (opposite). An increase in natural light has been made possible thanks to the removal of suspended ceilings and partition walls. Highlights include Alexander Nasmyth's painting of Robert Burns, and Robert Adamson and David Octavius Hill's 19th-century photo of a Newhaven fishwife. The magnificent suite of galleries on the top floor (Room 10; above) is not be missed.

1 Queen Street, T 624 6200, www.nationalgalleries.org

14.00 The Dogs
David Ramsden's trio of Edinburgh
restaurants – gastropub The Dogs,
seafood-focused Seadogs (T 225 8028)
and Italian-influenced Amore Dogs
(T 220 5155) – have real bite. The
original is the best, serving truly great
modern Scottish food in a first-floor
Georgian apartment. Such unaffected
dining is hard to find in the city.
110 Hanover Street, T 220 1208

16.00 Ingleby Gallery

The largest private contemporary art gallery outside London, the Ingleby was founded in 1998. Despite now being one of the grandes dames of the Edinburgh art scene, the gallery has a freshness about it, partly due to a move to a larger site in 2008. Since setting up shop in a former nightclub behind Waverley Station, owners Florence and Richard Ingleby have created a space suited to the tranquil appreciation of artists such as Peter Liversidge, Alison Watt, James Hugonin and the late Ian Hamilton Finlay, as well as collaborative installations like 'Gravity's Rainbow' (above). Don't miss the gallery's Billboard for Edinburgh project, which uses the building's hoarding as a space for public art.

15 Calton Road, T 556 4441,
www.inglebygallery.com

19.00 Castle Terrace

This recent city-centre project from the team behind The Kitchin (see p058) won a Michelin 'Rising Star' award within its first year. Chef Dominic Jack, rather than Tom Kitchin, is at the helm but, like its sister establishment, the restaurant's philosophy is 'from nature to plate', with much of the produce sourced in Scotland and exquisitely presented. The difference between the two restaurants is in the style of cooking, which at Castle Terrace leans towards classic French cuisine rather than Kitchin's earthier inclinations. The decor – purple and grey tartan chairs, a gilded ceiling and shimmery flowered wallpaper – plays to a home crowd that enjoys a bit of bling on a big night out, a promise Castle Terrace fulfils enjoyably. *33-35 Castle Terrace, T 229 1222, www.castleterracerestaurant.com*

URBAN LIFE
CAFÉS, RESTAURANTS, BARS AND NIGHTCLUBS

Edinburgh's culinary scene has transformed over the past decade. No longer the poor cousin to its rival Glasgow, it has steadily gained a reputation as one of the best cities in the UK for eating out. Five of its chefs – Martin Wishart (see p059), Tom Kitchin (see p058), Jeff Bland at The Balmoral's in-house restaurant Number One (1 Princes Street, T 557 6727), Paul Kitching (see p042) and Tony Borthwick of The Plumed Horse (50-54 Henderson Street, T 554 5556) – hold a Michelin star apiece. Three of their restaurants cluster in the gentrified port quarter of Leith.

As the headline acts have won plaudits, a fine supporting cast has stepped up to the plate. French-inspired brasserie The Honours (see p059) was booked solid within hours of opening in July 2011. And authentic French eateries, like L'Escargot Bleu (56 Broughton Street, T 557 1600) and La Garrigue (31 Jeffrey Street, T 557 3032), are thriving. Dining in Edinburgh can also be enchantingly romantic, as you'll discover at The Witchery's restaurant (see p022).

Although you'll never be far from liquid refreshment in Edinburgh, you'll need to choose your pubs with care. Most are welcoming, but some can be sniffy to non-locals and others have lost their charm. Bars are less risky: Bramble (see p054) is the drinking den du jour and The Voodoo Rooms (see p062) draws a clued-up crowd to its live music and glam surrounds.
For full addresses, see Resources.

Ondine

Since this pescatarian dream ticket opened in 2009, no seafood lover has been able to set foot in the Scottish capital without a visit to Ondine. Headed by Edinburgh-born chef Roy Brett, who has worked with Rick Stein, the restaurant breaks with the local habit of eating deep-fried fish and potatoes out of disposable plastic boxes and instead serves the most sophisticated fish and shellfish in the city. Take a pew at the horseshoe-shaped crustacean bar and feast on fresh oysters, lobster, clams and langoustines. Or book a table and tuck into grilled lemon sole, sea bream curry or, if you must have your food deep-fried, a peppy squid tempura. Every sliver of seafood served is accredited by the Marine Stewardship Council (MSC). *2 George IV Bridge, T 226 1888, www.ondinerestaurant.co.uk*

21212

Once you've mastered the name (it refers to the menu – a choice of two dishes, then a single set dish, followed by a choice of two more dishes; you get the idea), you'll need to fathom the decor. Royal Terrace is one of the city's Georgian jewels, and 21212 has taken the opulence and run with it. Edinburgh's answer to Louis XIV, it features expensively papered walls and ripplingly luxurious banquettes. And the food?

Handing over responsibility to chef-owner Paul Kitching is liberating. Dishes may read like crazed shopping lists – 'pulsating lamb' with spicy melon and sweet potato, smoked bacon crisps, pease pudding, barley, olives, pink peppercorns and rosemary cream – but the reward is one of Edinburgh's most entertaining meals.
3 Royal Terrace, T 523 1030,
www.21212restaurant.co.uk

Porto & Fi

Edinburgh has many places in which to enjoy a traditional breakfast, but few for brunch. Or it didn't before Porto & Fi, which serves a morning menu (all day on Sundays) that runs the full spectrum from porridge to eggs Benedict via French toast and almond croissants. In spring 2011, the original in Leith (above) was joined by a second branch, Porto & Fi On The Mound (T 225 9494), in North Bank Street. Both venues share a twee-free aesthetic, and the newcomer to the Mound brightens up exposed brick with scarlet pendant lights and paintwork the colour of cut grass. The lofty reputation of its older sibling meant that Porto & Fi's first city-centre venture won a diverse following for its crowd-pleasing menu almost before it opened. *47 Newhaven Main Street, T 551 1900, www.portofi.com*

Peter's Yard

Foster + Partners' redevelopment of the former Royal Infirmary (now known as Quartermile) may be uninspiring, but one of its redeeming features is this café/ bakery. The pale, clean-lined interiors by Norrgavel provide a refreshing change from the numerous boho coffee bars that litter the city. Founded by Swedish master baker Jan Hedh, Peter's Yard entices you through its glass doors with a pile of artisanal breads on the counter. Inside, the café offers Scandinavian-style treats, a superb lunch menu, mouthwatering cakes and desserts, homemade conserves, gourmet chocolate and the best coffee in town.
Quartermile, 27 Simpson Loan,
T 228 5876, www.petersyard.com

The Outsider

A comfortable, unfussy interior and wallet-friendly prices helped put this eaterie on the map. The second of owner Malcolm Innes' brasseries (first came The Apartment, T 228 6456), The Outsider serves generous portions of wholesome, tasty food, including some innovative fish dishes. The convivial atmosphere and castle views make this a great destination for both lunch and dinner.

If you're in a large group, make sure you secure the snug, while the smaller tables at the back are the spot for tête-à-têtes. Outsider or not, with some formidable new competition in the shape of The Honours (see p059) and Hotel du Vin's central Edinburgh outpost (11 Bristo Place, T 247 4900), Innes' restaurant will need to stay on top of its game.
15-16 George IV Bridge, T 226 3131

The Shore Bar & Restaurant

One of the country's first gastropubs, The Shore opened its doors more than 30 years ago and has matured into a much-loved fixture on Leith's waterfront, its lively bar and cosy dining room unchanging from year to year. Now owned by a local restaurant group, the kitchen's focus is on seafood, sharing the menu with gastropub staples such as slow-roasted lamb shanks. With full menus available from noon until last orders at night, an unhurried, easygoing atmosphere persists here. Befitting The Shore's casual appeal, plenty of wines are available by the glass. And, for younger diners, children's portions are offered with a smile.
3 The Shore, T 553 5080,
www.fishersbistros.co.uk

The Saint
Soothingly decorated with whitewashed walls, vintage lamps, fresh flowers, wooden tables, comfy armchairs and handwritten menus, this diminutive bar and restaurant is more a place to enjoy a quiet evening à deux than a late-night drinking session, not least because of the well-priced modern British menu.
44 St Stephen Street, T 225 9009, www.thesaintedinburgh.co.uk

Bia Bistrot

There's nothing like bagging a table in a popular neighbourhood restaurant to make you feel as though you've found a direct short cut to the heart of the city, and this eaterie, in Edinburgh's wealthy Morningside area, is just that. A find for visiting foodies, and with host of regular punters, Bia Bistrot punches above its weight with inventive but relaxed cooking at reasonable prices. Bia means 'food' in Irish Gaelic, and the ethos here is one of openness and conviviality, aimed at providing a laidback atmosphere. That's partly achieved through dedication to quality local ingredients, with fish supplied by Welch in Newhaven, Carrolls Heritage potatoes from Northumberland and cheeses by Iain J Mellis (see p080). *19 Colinton Road, T 452 8453, www.biabistrot.co.uk*

Restaurant at The Bonham

This venue has achieved what can be a tough ask for an in-house eaterie: an identity quite separate to that of the hotel in which it's based. It ranks as one of Edinburgh's most highly regarded restaurants, which is testament to the skills of its long-serving, Brittany-born head chef Michel Bouyer. The cooking stays close to Bouyer's homeland but plunders local produce, as seen in dishes such as seared scallops with ham hock-stuffed pig's trotter and confit grapes, and pan-fried Aberdeen Angus fillet of beef with fondant potato, seared foie gras and cep jus. Bouyer also caters brilliantly to the city's sweet tooth; leave plenty of room for his signature brownies, which are served with coffee.
35 Drumsheugh Gardens, T 274 7444,
www.thebonham.com

Sweet Melindas

There's an intimacy and a knowing buzz here that you won't find in any other Old Town eaterie. Tucked away in the residential quarter of Marchmont, Sweet Melindas is a tiny fish restaurant, with a charming decor of white panelled walls and black-and-white photos. Owner and chef Kevin O'Connor is serious about making everything from scratch, from the soda bread to the chocolate truffles, and the short menu changes daily, according to the catch bought at Eddie's Seafood Market next door. A fairly priced wine list and devilishly good desserts help ensure a loyal clientele. *11 Roseneath Street, T 229 7953, www.sweetmelindas.co.uk*

Bramble

With just a touch of the speakeasy about it, Bramble is easily the best bar in town just now. Its smoke-and-mirrors interior, so small that you assume there must be another room back there (there's not), draws a mixed crowd of regulars and in-the-know out-of-towners. Pile into this underground tavern late in the evening to recline on worn leather armchairs or benches laid with plump cushions, and chew the fat in flickering candlelight while the DJ does his thing, the party rides on and beautiful, no-nonsense staff mix the best cocktails in town; try the signature Bramble and you'll see what we mean. The catch? During university term time you'll share it with bevies of high-spirited and high-rolling tweed-blazered students. *16a Queen Street, T 226 6343, www.bramblebar.co.uk*

Kay's Bar

Tucked away in what looks like a detached cottage in the heart of the New Town, Kay's is about as authentic as a pub can get. Locals, mostly men of a certain age, have earned their places around the bar, where handlebar-moustached barman Fraser Gillespie dispenses local ales and a selection of about 50 malts. Friendly and welcoming, the pub serves a top-notch lunch of haggis, neeps (swede) and tatties, but really comes into its own on quiet winter evenings, when the fire's roaring and you can play a game of Scrabble in the back library. *39 Jamaica Street, T 225 1858, www.kaysbar.co.uk*

The Canny Mans
Famed for its brusque service and ban
on mobile phones, backpackers and
credit cards, The Canny Mans is one of
the city's most treasured drinking dens,
despite its out-of-the-way location.
The smorgasbord-inspired menu is as
busy as the interior, which is rammed
to the rafters with curiosities. This place
is quirky, full of character and fun.
237 Morningside Road, T 447 1484

The Kitchin

Proprietor and head chef Tom Kitchin draws a serious crowd to his Edinburgh restaurant, located in a uniform row of eateries and bars in Leith's Commercial Quay. The Kitchin caused a flurry of excitement when it opened in 2006, and a Michelin star awarded just seven months later confirmed the hype was justified. The cuisine features mainly seasonal Scottish produce, prepared using French techniques. Despite the elegant interior, the place has never quite taken off as the glam haunt it was perhaps intended to be, and is best suited to business or more formal dining occasions.

78 Commercial Quay, T 555 1755, www.thekitchin.com

The Honours

For more than a decade, Martin Wishart's eponymous Leith restaurant (54 The Shore, T 553 3557) has enchanted foodies from Edinburgh and beyond. In July 2011, the Michelin-starred chef's acolytes gained a new place of worship, when The Honours opened just off Queen Street. The brasserie, helmed by right-hand man Paul Tamburrini, draws punchy flavours from Scottish produce, with dishes such as Scrabster halibut on spicy lentils with pomme purée. The three-course lunch prix-fixe menu is fairly priced. For the interior design, Wishart turned to long-standing collaborators Ian Smith Design. Rather than emulate Wishart's subdued fine-dining restaurant, Smith got out his set square for a bold, geometric look. *58a North Castle Street, T 220 2513, www.thehonours.co.uk*

Oloroso

This restaurant's rooftop setting and simple but tasteful decor – crisp white table linen set against sleek leather chairs – single it out as one of the best-designed eateries in town. Located on the fourth floor of an unassuming building, its discreet location enhances the allure. The work of Richard Murphy Architects, Oloroso's sophisticated interior impresses from the minute you step out of the lift,

and owner and head chef Tony Singh has devised a slick menu to match. Alongside a permanent grill menu of steak, veal and seafood is a seasonal selection of mains, such as pan-fried fillet of sea bass with compote of squash and apple, served with citrus and prawn sauce. Alternatively, call in for a drink at Oloroso's fine lounge bar. *33 Castle Street, T 226 7614, www.oloroso.co.uk*

INSIDER'S GUIDE

ROSAMUND WEST, EDITOR

In this city of festivals, Rosamund West's job as editor of *The Skinny*, Edinburgh's independent culture and listings magazine, is a front-line role. 'Edinburgh's scene can be insular,' she says, 'we try to prise it open a bit.' Her weekends often start by sharing croissants with her artist partner at The Manna House (22-24 Easter Road, T 652 2349), a bakery in Leith run by former pastry chefs. This is followed by a stroll in Holyrood Park: 'That this piece of countryside, with a ruined castle, sits in the heart of the city still surprises me.' Hungry for art, they wander up the Royal Mile to The Fruitmarket Gallery (45 Market Street, T 225 2383) or along the Water of Leith walkway to the Scottish National Gallery of Modern Art (75 Belford Road, T 624 6200).

'Time permitting, we might check out some shops,' says West. 'Some great boutiques, such as Moleta Munro (see p084), are tucked away in the Old Town. Godiva on the Grassmarket (9 West Port, T 221 9212) is a haven for vintage and unique garments by local designers. It is very supportive of new fashion and jewellery graduates.' Her favourite food stop is Chop Chop (248 Morrison Street, T 221 1155), a Chinese restaurant 'famous for its steamed or fried dumplings'. A perfect evening concludes with live music at Limbo in The Voodoo Rooms (19a West Register Street, T 556 7060), all gilt, mirrors and Grey Goose martinis.
For full addresses, see Resources.

ARCHITOUR

A GUIDE TO EDINBURGH'S ICONIC BUILDINGS

The fact that Edinburgh is blessed with some of the finest historic buildings in the country makes it ideal for architourists, but for working architects based in the city it has been a huge burden. Up until 20 years ago, there was essentially a moratorium on changing the landscape in the centre, which was in danger of turning into a museum rather than the buzzing heart of a modern city. However, the 1990s brought a need for new office space and housing, and an easing of the draconian planning laws. It was acknowledged that the new could be successfully blended with the old, and the Scottish Storytelling Centre (see p073), Dovecot Studios' new tapestry centre (see p076) and Dance Base (see p092) have been praised for stitching threads of modernity into the old fabric.

Indeed, Edinburgh has grown so confident about modern architecture that it now boasts one of the most innovative contemporary structures in Britain today. The Scottish Parliament (see p070), the creation of the late Enric Miralles, was completed in 2004, and became a turning point for the city's built environment. Those who love it say that it gave Edinburgh a building to be proud of and opened up the architectural arena for a freer approach. Others regard the project as a disaster – three years late and over budget, by a whopping £380m, a fiasco matched only by the city's problematic, runaway tram project, which upturned Princes Street. *For full addresses, see Resources.*

National Museum of Scotland

Hot on the heels of the refurbishment of the Scottish National Portrait Gallery (see p034) came a major overhaul of the Victorian section of the National Museum of Scotland (formerly the Royal Museum). The £46m project, completed in 2011, saw the oldest part of the country's flagship museum (above) restored to its glass-ceilinged glory by Balfour Beatty and specialists Beck Interiors. No longer an odd partnership between a slightly careworn relic and the bold architectural extension attached to it in 1998 by Benson & Forsyth (overleaf), the redevelopment has seen both buildings combine to offer more public space, updated displays, an interactive technology zone, and a new entrance hall, café and shop.
Chambers Street, T 0300 123 6789, www.nms.ac.uk

Royal Commonwealth Pool

Most locals tend to ignore this brutalist building and head straight to the Olympic-size swimming pool inside. We'd advise you to linger and admire the view before taking your dip. Designed by Robert Matthew, a protégé of the great Scottish architect Basil Spence, the Category-A-listed complex was constructed as one of the venues for the 1970 Commonwealth Games, and has been heavily used by the public ever since. The 'Commie', as it's known locally, is due to reopen after a two-and-a-half-year upgrade and refurbishment in spring 2012, partly serving as a top-level training facility for the country's Olympic-standard swimmers. *21 Dalkeith Road, T 667 7211, www.edinburghleisure.co.uk*

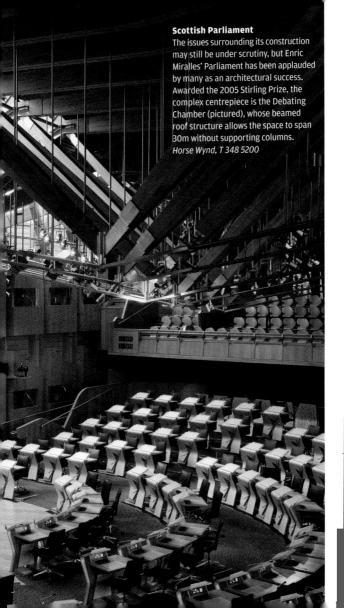

Scottish Parliament
The issues surrounding its construction may still be under scrutiny, but Enric Miralles' Parliament has been applauded by many as an architectural success. Awarded the 2005 Stirling Prize, the complex centrepiece is the Debating Chamber (pictured), whose beamed roof structure allows the space to span 30m without supporting columns.
Horse Wynd, T 348 5200

Old College

The home of Edinburgh University's School of Law took a century (1789-1887) to finish, with architect Robert Adam's brothers, James and William, followed by William Playfair, supervising the build after his death, and Sir Robert Rowand Anderson adding the dome in 1887. A dramatic stone arch announces the entrance to Old College, and although its attractive courtyard was being used as a car park up until 2010, even that couldn't take away from the impact of Adam's landmark. Now, however, a grassed quadrangle proposed by Playfair in his original design, never realised due to lack of funds, is finally coming to fruition through a plan from local firm Simpson & Brown that is sympathetic to Playfair's original vision. *South Bridge, www.law.ed.ac.uk/tour*

Scottish Storytelling Centre

In one of Britain's most protected urban zones, the Netherbow, perched on the Royal Mile and adjacent to the listed John Knox House, which dates to 1470, Malcolm Fraser Architects masterfully set the modern next to the ancient. The Scottish Storytelling Centre is a scheme that aims to revive a dying oral tradition. Take a peek inside to witness how the light, informal interior spaces of the 21st-century building juxtapose effortlessly with the 15th-century house next door. The contemporary bell tower incorporates a plaque, once mounted over the archway of the ancient Netherbow gate to the city, and above which the heads of executed criminals were impaled; and the Netherbow Bell, which tolled as prisoners were led to their deaths.
43-45 High Street, T 556 9579,
www.scottishstorytellingcentre.co.uk

Randolph Crescent
Drawing from experience gained on
previous Georgian New Town projects
Moray Place and Ainslie Place, the Earl
of Moray and architect James Gillespie
Graham created a softer, less uniform
structure for Randolph Crescent, built
between 1822 and 1855. With its fewer
straight lines and a less austere feel,
little wonder that it is a frequently
used backdrop for period dramas.

Dovecot Studios

This highly regarded but little-known gallery blends the city's past and present to great effect. The gallery was previously a swimming pool, in use from 1885 until the 1990s, when dereliction meant the first public baths in Edinburgh had to be closed. To the rescue flew Dovecot Studios, a world-class contemporary tapestry firm, which celebrates its centenary in 2012. Dovecot moved in after a reinvention of the space in 2009, and tapestry-weaving is at the heart of the building. The site is also home to IC: Innovative Craft, which works with artists, makers, curators and arts organisations to provide exhibitions and events that explore craft in the 21st century. In 2011, the café Stag Espresso (T 07590 728 974) opened on site.
10 Infirmary Street, T 550 3660,
www.dovecotstudios.com

Royal Botanic Garden Edinburgh

A perennial favourite of visitors to Edinburgh, what was founded in the 17th century as a physic garden now extends over 70 acres of painstakingly landscaped grounds just north of the city centre. An imaginative exhibition and events programme engages with local communities to keep the public, as well as plant buffs, returning. The opening of a visitor centre at the garden's sedum-roofed John Hope Gateway (pictured) in 2009 has reinvigorated the visitor experience. Named after John Hope, RBGE's royal keeper from 1761 to 1786, this award-winning low-carbon building by Edward Cullinan Architects incorporates a shop, exhibition space, nursery and eaterie. *Arboretum Place, T 552 7171, www.rbge.org.uk*

SHOPPING

THE BEST RETAIL THERAPY AND WHAT TO BUY

Princes Street and George Street vie for the title of Edinburgh's main shopping drag. Between the two stands Jenners (48 Princes Street, T 225 2442), Scotland's stateliest department store. Nearby, Harvey Nichols (30-34 St Andrew Square, T 524 8388) has five floors packed with Marc Jacobs, Chloé et al, while Louis Vuitton (1-2 Multrees Walk North, T 652 5900) and Emporio Armani (25 Multrees Walk, T 523 1580) keep label-loving locals satisfied.

For specialist boutiques, the steep and winding cobbled Victoria Street is home to several gems, including the joke shop Aha Ha Ha (99 West Bow, T 220 5252), IJ Mellis Cheesemonger (30a Victoria Street, T 226 6215), art bookshop Analogue (see p085) and tailor Walker Slater (see p086). Vintage fans should check out Armstrongs (83 Grassmarket, T 220 5557) and Godiva Boutique (see p062), while you'll find the most covetable furniture at Tangram Furnishers (33-37 Jeffrey Street, T 556 6551) and Concrete Wardrobe (50a Broughton Street, T 558 7130).

If you're on the hunt for edible treats, the Saturday farmers' market (9am to 2pm) on Castle Terrace is a must, as is a visit to German baker Falko Konditormeister (185 Bruntsfield Place, T 656 0763) and the Edinburgh institution Valvona & Crolla (19 Elm Row, T 556 6066), which also owns VinCaffè (11 Multrees Walk, T 557 0088), ideally located for a post-shopping coffee stop. *For full addresses, see Resources.*

Bruichladdich Scotch Whisky

One of the most exciting independent craft distillers in Scotland, Bruichladdich dates from 1881, but fell into disuse before a rescue party led by Mark Reynier arrived in 2000. Reynier's whisky is known for its limited bottlings, and purity; it's not coloured or chill-filtered. And the forward-looking product design helps single-malt shed its whiskery image. Islay's only organic single-malt, The Organic 2010 (above; £36), is, according to Bruichladdich's master distiller, Jim McEwan, 'an elegant, composed and stylish young spirit'. Taste it in Edinburgh at the Whiski Rooms (T 225 7224), an unfussy venue with 250 whiskies in stock.
Isle of Islay, T 01496 850 190
www.bruichladdich.com

Anta
For a tartan keepsake, skip the shops flogging cheap tat on the Royal Mile and hit Anta, for everything from porridge bowls to wool rugs. Here, you'll swap the bright red, yellow and blue of Royal Stewart for chic, Farrow & Ball-friendly tones: Highland heather mauve, Glencoe skies grey, and clootie dumpling taupe.
73 Grassmarket, T 225 9096, www.anta.co.uk

Moleta Munro

This contemporary design store run by Justin Baddon and wife Juliet Moleta blew a fresh, light breeze through Edinburgh's retail scene when it opened up behind Waverley Station, in the Old Town, in 2007. An interiors shop that offered both carefully sourced pieces from big-name European brands and up-and-coming Scottish designers, but sold them in a way that was warm, welcoming and devoid of snootiness, was just what Edinburgh needed. And it's worked. The couple's stock of furniture, lighting, lifestyle products and accessories continues to draw a loyal following, as does their modernist Timber House (see p096) holiday home on the Isle of Skye, which is available to rent (ask in-store for details). *4 Jeffrey Street, T 557 4800, www.moletamunro.com*

Analogue

It's not just because it stocks Wallpaper* City Guides among its set of design, art and architecture titles that we've included Analogue here. Originally opened on Victoria Street in 2001, but recently moved to new premises just around the corner, the shop sells a daring edit of contemporary-culture books, magazines, music, T-shirts and prints. More than just a store, it is a place to get inspired. Owners Russell Ferguson and Julie Nichol actively promote young illustrators and graphic designers, run occasional talks and exhibitions, publish a series of art 'zines and produce limited-edition screen prints by local artists. *39 Candlemaker Row, T 220 0601, www.analoguebooks.co.uk*

Walker Slater

If the endless tourist junk and scratchy wool have put you off Scottish tailoring, your faith will be swiftly restored here. Walker Slater specialises in casual and formalwear – high-quality wool jumpers, cords, tweed jackets and bespoke suits from its own collection, as well as select British brands such as Albert Thurston. *20 Victoria Street, T 220 2636, www.walkerslater.com*

SPORTS AND SPAS

WORK OUT, CHILL OUT OR JUST WATCH

Edinburgh is the stepping stone to a host of country pursuits all over Scotland. As a result, the city has some of the best sports accessories shops in the country. Those heading out to hunt can get fully kitted out at Dickson & MacNaughton (21 Frederick Street, T 225 4218). Scotland's rivers attract fishermen from far and wide, and anglers will find all they need at Gamefish (6a Howe Street, T 220 6465). Golfers who are on their way to St Andrews or the links courses in East Lothian should visit the Edinburgh Golf Centre (58 Dalry Road, T 337 5888).

Within the city itself, the architecturally acclaimed Dance Base (see p092) studios in the Grassmarket opened its doors in 2001 and has been instrumental in getting locals moving; the Edinburgh International Climbing Arena (see p093) arrived in the suburbs in 2007; and the Royal Commonwealth Pool (see p068), already enjoying its new gym, fitness studios and diving pool, has been renovated to Olympic standard for Britain's aquatic competitors. The best pampering option in town is the Sheraton's One Spa (see p094), but Hotel Missoni (see p026) now offers some fresh competition. Edinburgh's major spectator sports are football and rugby. Football may draw the more partisan crowds, especially when local sides Hibs or Hearts play Glasgow's Rangers or Celtic, but rugby boasts a far superior stadium in Murrayfield (see p090). *For full addresses, see Resources.*

Glenogle Swim Centre

A paean to the Victorian predilection for self-improvement, this is one of several late 19th-century and early 20th-century swimming pools still in operation across the city. Of those that are accessible to the public, council-run Glenogle Baths (as it's known locally) is the most central, sandwiched between the Georgian splendour of Saxe-Coburg Place and the quirky B-listed 'colony' houses off Glenogle Road that were built as a philanthropic endeavour. Go for a swim and you can admire the baths' architecture from the water. Local campaigners in the lead-up to the site's 2010 refurbishment persuaded the council to keep the glass ceiling, gallery and poolside cubicles that give a dip here so much atmosphere. *Glenogle Road, T 343 6376, www.edinburghleisure.co.uk*

Murrayfield

With a capacity of 67,500, Murrayfield is one of Britain's largest and most atmospheric stadiums. The ground has hosted rugby matches since 1925, and the current, structurally expressive bowl was designed by Connor Milligan Architects and completed in 1994. The impressive arena comes into its own for international fixtures, such as Six Nations ties, for which tickets are like gold dust. In addition to rugby, American football and The Highland Games have been played here. It has even hosted a youth rally to welcome the Pope, and is a popular venue for music concerts. Behind-the-scenes tours take in the pitch, dressing rooms and hospitality suites.
Roseburn Street, T 346 5000,
www.scottishrugby.org

Dance Base

From Scottish reeling to hip hop and salsa, dancing got a huge lift in Edinburgh thanks to this building, designed by Malcolm Fraser Architects. Wedged between the Grassmarket's cafés and pubs, few would have had the vision, or indeed ambition, to create something quite so unique on this dog-legged site. It is, however, the studio's incorporation of an existing structure and exploitation of the striking castle views, via the large expanses of glass used for the roof, that has drawn most praise. The range of drop-in classes, held in four elegant, timber-clad studios, is impressive, so this may be your chance to try out some burlesque or belly dancing.

14-16 Grassmarket, T 225 5525,
www.dancebase.co.uk

EICA

As the largest indoor climbing facility in the world, the Edinburgh International Climbing Arena (EICA) won a place in the record books for its hometown of Ratho, 20 minutes west of Edinburgh. The state-of-the-art venue is the creation of Edinburgh climbers Rab Anderson and Duncan McCallum, who teamed up with architect David Taylor to create a five-storey structure built into a 30.5m disused quarry. This engineering feat means the centre not only offers 3,000 sq m of artificial climbing, but it is the only indoor complex in the world that boasts natural rock walls. There is also an aerial rope course, an adventure sports gym, a health club, café and film auditorium, plus various bouldering problems to solve.

South Platt Hill, Ratho, Newbridge, T 333 6333, www.eica-ratho.com

One Spa
Bypass the unsightly Sheraton Grand
Hotel and head for the connecting One
Spa. This luxurious retreat, opened
in 2001, offers saunas, steam rooms
and a good range of treatments, but
the pièce de résistance is the saltwater
rooftop hydropool (pictured). Open all
year, its temperature is a balmy 35°C.
8 Conference Square, T 221 7777,
www.onespa.com

ESCAPES

WHERE TO GO IF YOU WANT TO LEAVE TOWN

Edinburgh's modest size means that getting out is quick and easy. A short taxi ride can transport you to dramatic scenery, while further afield, by car or train, are breathtaking surroundings and myriad outdoor activities, especially around Peebles to the south.

Musselburgh is a quaint seaside fishing town that is convenient for a day trip. Less contaminated by amusement arcades and chip shops than its larger neighbour Portobello, it is home to one of the best gelaterias in Europe, S Luca (32-38 High Street, T 665 2237), open for business since 1908 and alone worth the six-mile journey.

Self-catering properties are a perfect way to explore Scotland's hills, beaches and lochs. Chic options abound: in the north-west, Shore Croft in the village of Mellon Charles can be booked via www.underthethatch.co.uk, while craft and design retailer Papa Stour (T 07922 771 424) worked magic on rustic Callakille cottage (Applecross, T 01456 486 358). Corrour (www.corrour.co.uk) has lodges – some decorated by Suzy Hoodless – in the Highlands, about 40 minutes by train from Fort William. But the Isle of Skye has the best selection, with the Timber House (Skinidin, T 557 4800), from the founders of Moleta Munro (see p084), and The Shed (see p100) among many more small-but-perfectly-formed hideaways. The highly regarded Three Chimneys restaurant with rooms (Colbost, T 01470 511 258) is a key part of Skye's appeal. *For full addresses, see Resources.*

Jupiter Artland, Wilkieston

Open from mid-May until mid-September, this art gallery and sculpture park, half an hour from Edinburgh by car, opened in 2009. Commissioning many of the big names in contemporary art to make work in situ in one fairly compact space, co-owner Nicky Wilson shows what can be done with vision – and private investment. Fans of Charles Jencks' *Landform* at the Scottish National Gallery of Modern Art (see p062) can now admire his vast installation *Life Mounds* (overleaf), a series of swirling earthwork knolls at Jupiter. It forms a mighty full-stop to a tour of large-scale pieces by Andy Goldsworthy, Antony Gormley, Cornelia Parker, Marc Quinn and more, including Jim Lambie's *ZOBOP (Fluorescent)* (above). *Bonnington House Steadings, T 01506 889 900, www.jupiterartland.org*

Life Mounds, Jupiter Artland

The Shed, Isle of Skye
Set in native woodland on Skye's west coast, what sets The Shed apart from other retreats is its contemporary interior by Dualchas Building Design. Despite the pared-down aesthetic, a wood-burning stove warms the light, open spaces. The nearest airport is Inverness, three hours away by car.
Tokavaig, T 01471 855 407,
www.skyeshed.com

The Falkirk Wheel

This engineering solution connecting the Forth and Clyde Canal with the Union Canal has not only restored navigability across Scotland, the *Return of the Jedi*-like structure has also become a slightly offbeat tourist attraction. Opened in 2002, the world's first rotating boat lift replaces the former, tedious system of 11 locks. Boats entering the upper gondola are lowered, along with the water they float in, to the basin below. At the same time, an equal weight is lifted in the lower gondola. Don't get it? Take a trip yourself, starting at the Visitor Centre. Boats are first gracefully lifted by the gondola 35m up to the Union Canal and then sail through the Roughcastle Tunnel, under the historic Antonine Wall, before returning to the Wheel to be rotated down again.

Lime Road, Tamfourhill, Falkirk, T 08700 500 208, www.thefalkirkwheel.co.uk

NOTES
SKETCHES AND MEMOS

RESOURCES
CITY GUIDE DIRECTORY

A

Aha Ha Ha 080
 99 West Bow
 T 220 5252

Amore Dogs 036
 109 Hanover Street
 T 220 5155
 www.amoredogs.co.uk

Analogue 085
 39 Candlemaker Row
 T 220 0601
 www.analoguebooks.co.uk

Anta 082
 73 Grassmarket
 T 225 9096
 www.anta.co.uk

The Apartment 046
 7-13 Barclay Place
 T 228 6456

Armstrongs 080
 83 Grassmarket
 T 220 5557
 www.armstrongsvintage.co.uk

B

Bia Bistrot 050
 19 Colinton Road
 T 452 8453
 www.biabistrot.co.uk

Bramble 054
 16a Queen Street
 T 226 6343
 www.bramblebar.co.uk

Bruichladdich 081
 Isle of Islay
 T 01496 850 190
 www.bruichladdich.com

C

The Canny Mans 056
 237 Morningside Road
 T 447 1484

Castle Terrace 039
 33-35 Castle Terrace
 T 229 1222
 www.castleterracerestaurant.com

Chop Chop 062
 248 Morrison Street
 T 221 1155
 www.chop-chop.co.uk

Concrete Wardrobe 080
 50a Broughton Street
 T 558 7130

D

Dance Base 092
 14-16 Grassmarket
 T 225 5525
 www.dancebase.co.uk

Dickson & MacNaughton 088
 21 Frederick Street
 T 225 4218
 www.dicksonandmacnaughton.com

The Dogs 036
 110 Hanover Street
 T 220 1208
 www.thedogsonline.co.uk

Dovecot Studios 076
 10 Infirmary Street
 T 550 3660
 www.dovecotstudios.com

E

Edinburgh Castle 010
 Castle Hill
 T 225 9846
 www.edinburghcastle.gov.uk

HOTELS

ADDRESSES AND ROOM RATES

The Balmoral 016
Room rates:
double, from £380
1 Princes Street
T 556 2414
www.thebalmoralhotel.com

Callakille cottage 096
Room rates:
double, from £465 per week
Applecross
Wester Ross
T 01456 486 358
www.wildernesscottages.co.uk

The Glasshouse 024
Room rates:
double, from £150;
Executive Room, £350;
Suite, £450
2 Greenside Place
T 525 8200
www.theetoncollection.com

The Howard 017
Room rates:
double, from £200;
Abercromby Suite, £380
34 Great King Street
T 557 3500
www.thehoward.com

Hotel Missoni 026
Room rates:
double, from £190;
Room 507, £235;
Suite D'Argento, £1,500
1 George IV Bridge
T 220 6666
www.hotelmissoni.com

94DR 018
Room rates:
double, from £100;
Bowmore Room, £160
94 Dalkeith Road
T 662 9265
www.94dr.com

One Royal Circus 028
Room rates:
double, from £138
1 Royal Circus
T 625 6669
www.oneroyalcircus.com

Prestonfield 020
Room rates:
double, from £295;
Allan Ramsay Suite, £360
Priestfield Road
T 225 7800
www.prestonfield.com

The Scotsman 029
Room rates:
double, from £120;
Editor's Office, from £500;
Director's Suite, from £750;
Penthouse Suite, from £2,000
20 North Bridge
T 556 5565
www.thescotsmanhotel.co.uk

The Shed 100
Room rates:
price on request
Tokavaig
Isle of Skye
T 01471 855 407
www.skyeshed.com

Shore Croft 096
Room rates:
double, from £420 per week
Mellon Charles
Wester Ross
T 08445 005 101
www.underthethatch.co.uk

Three Chimneys Restaurant 096
Room rates:
double, £295
Colbost
Dunvegan
Isle of Skye
T 01470 511 258
www.threechimneys.co.uk

Tigerlily 030
Room rates:
double, £145;
Georgian Suite, from £425
125 George Street
T 225 5005
www.tigerlilyedinburgh.co.uk

Timber House 096
Room rates:
double, from £450 per week
Skinidin
Isle of Skye
T 557 4800
www.timberhouse-skye.co.uk

The Witchery 022
Room rates:
double, from £325;
Library Suite, £325;
Old Rectory, £325
Castlehill
The Royal Mile
T 225 5613
www.thewitchery.com

WALLPAPER* CITY GUIDES

Executive Editor
Rachael Moloney

Editor
Robin Barton

Authors
Alex Bagner
Rhiannon Batten

Art Director
Loran Stosskopf

Art Editor
Eriko Shimazaki
Designer
Mayumi Hashimoto
Map Illustrator
Russell Bell

Photography Editor
Sophie Corben
Deputy Photography Editor
Anika Burgess
Photography Assistant
Nabil Butt

Chief Sub-Editor
Nick Mee
Sub-Editor
Greg Hughes

Editorial Assistant
Emma Harrison

Intern
Claudia Chwalisz

**Wallpaper* Group
Editor-in-Chief**
Tony Chambers
Publishing Director
Gord Ray
Managing Editor
Jessica Diamond

Wallpaper* ® is a
registered trademark
of IPC Media Limited

First published 2008
Second edition (revised
and updated) 2012

All prices are correct at
the time of going to press,
but are subject to change.

Printed in China

PHAIDON

Phaidon Press Limited
Regent's Wharf
All Saints Street
London N1 9PA

Phaidon Press Inc
180 Varick Street
New York, NY 10014

Phaidon® is a registered
trademark of Phaidon
Press Limited

www.phaidon.com

A CIP Catalogue record for
this book is available from
the British Library.

© 2008 and 2012
IPC Media Limited

ISBN 978 0 7148 6301 6

PHOTOGRAPHERS

Benjamin Blossom
Edinburgh Castle,
pp010-011
McEwan Hall, p012
National Monument, p013
Forth Rail Bridge,
pp014-015
The Howard, p017
The Witchery, pp022-023
The Glasshouse,
p024, p025
One Royal Circus, p028
The Scotsman, p029
Tigerlily, pp030-031
Urban Angel, p033
Peter's Yard, p045
The Shore Bar &
Restaurant, p047
Restaurant at
The Bonham, p051
Sweet Melindas,
pp052-053
Kay's Bar, p055
The Canny Mans,
pp056-057
Oloroso, pp060-061
National Museum of
Scotland, pp066-067
Royal Commonwealth
Pool, pp068-069
Scottish Parliament,
pp070-071
Old College, p072

Scottish Storytelling
Centre, p073
Randolph Crescent,
pp074-075
Walker Slater, pp086-087
Murrayfield, pp090-091
One Spa, pp094-095

Matt Clayton
94DR, pp018-019
Prestonfield, p020, p021
Hotel Missoni, pp026-027
Scottish National Portrait
Gallery, p035
Castle Terrace, p039
Ondine, p041
21212, pp042-043
Porto & Fi, p044
The Saint, pp048-049
Bia Bistrot, p050
Bramble, p054
Rosamund West, p063
Dovecot Studios,
pp076-077
Royal Botanic Garden
Edinburgh, pp078-079
Anta, pp082-083
Moleta Munro, p084
Analogue, p085
Glenogle Swim
Centre, p089

**Jerry Driendl/
Getty Images**
Edinburgh city view,
inside front cover

**Keith Hunter
Photography**
Scottish National
Portrait Gallery, p034

Andrew Lee
The Shed, pp100-101

John McKenzie
Ingleby Gallery, p038

Peartree Digital
Bruichladdich The Organic
2010 whisky, p081

Allan Pollok-Morris
Jupiter Artland, p097,
pp098-099

EDINBURGH

A COLOUR-CODED GUIDE TO THE HOT 'HOODS

LEITH
Once a gritty port in north-east Edinburgh, the waterfront is now sought-after real estate

SOUTHSIDE/NEWINGTON
A sprawling borough characterised by green spaces, university buildings and theatres

NEW TOWN
James Craig's urban idyll is city planning at its finest, and a feast of Georgian architecture

OLD TOWN
Sidestep the tourist traps to marvel at the medieval splendour of this World Heritage Site

WEST END/TOLLCROSS/BRUNTSFIELD
Gentrifying fast, these zones are now home to the middle classes, chichi stores and delis

CANONGATE
A host of historic and modern landmarks are packed into this small corner of the city

For a full description of each neighbourhood, see the Introduction.
Featured venues are colour-coded, according to the district in which they are located.